LIVING THINGS IN THE ARCTIC

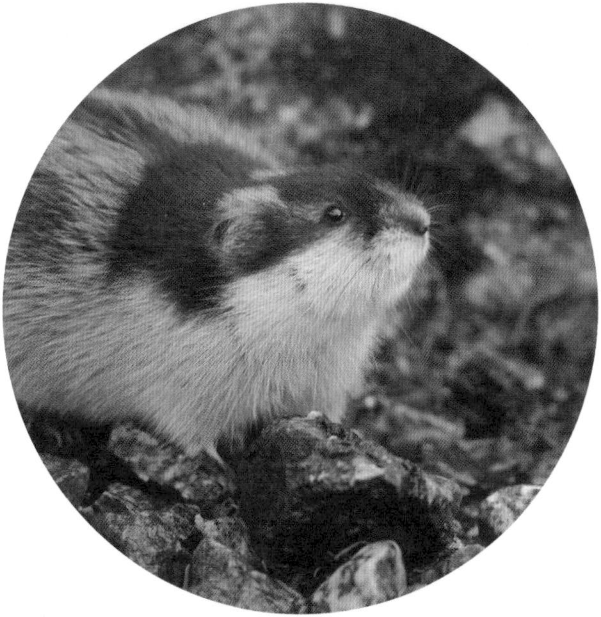

This is a raven.

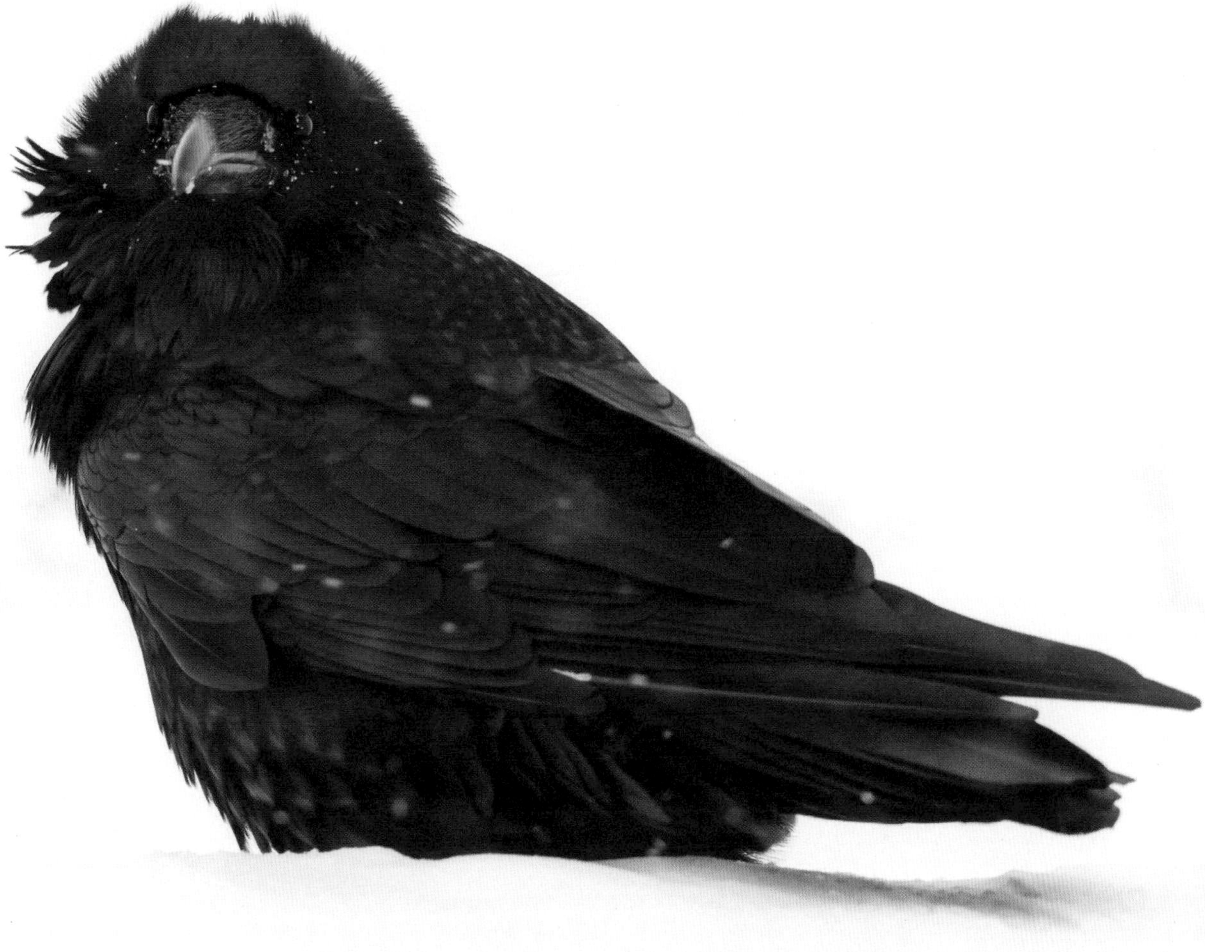

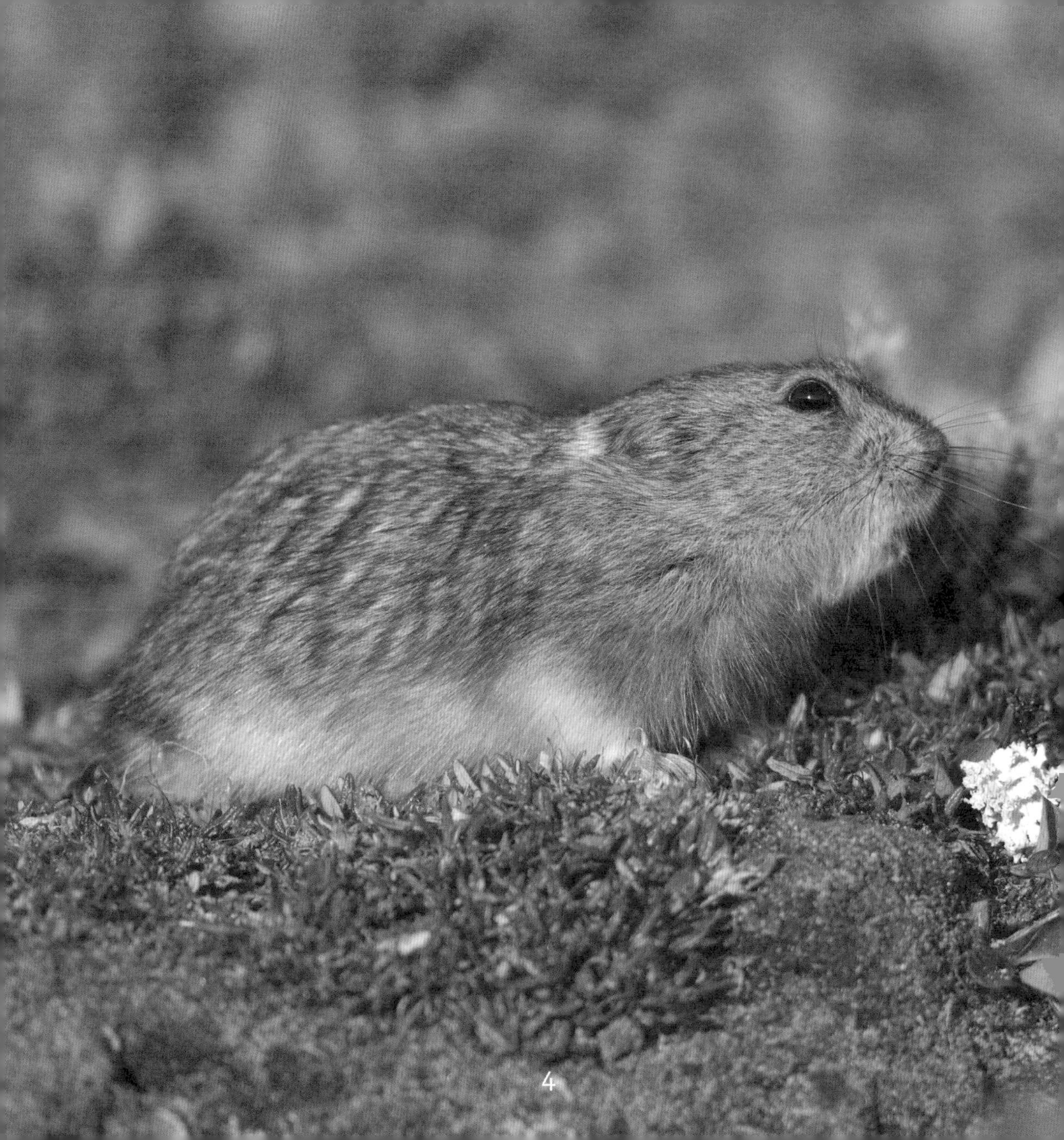

This is a lemming.

This is Arctic willow.

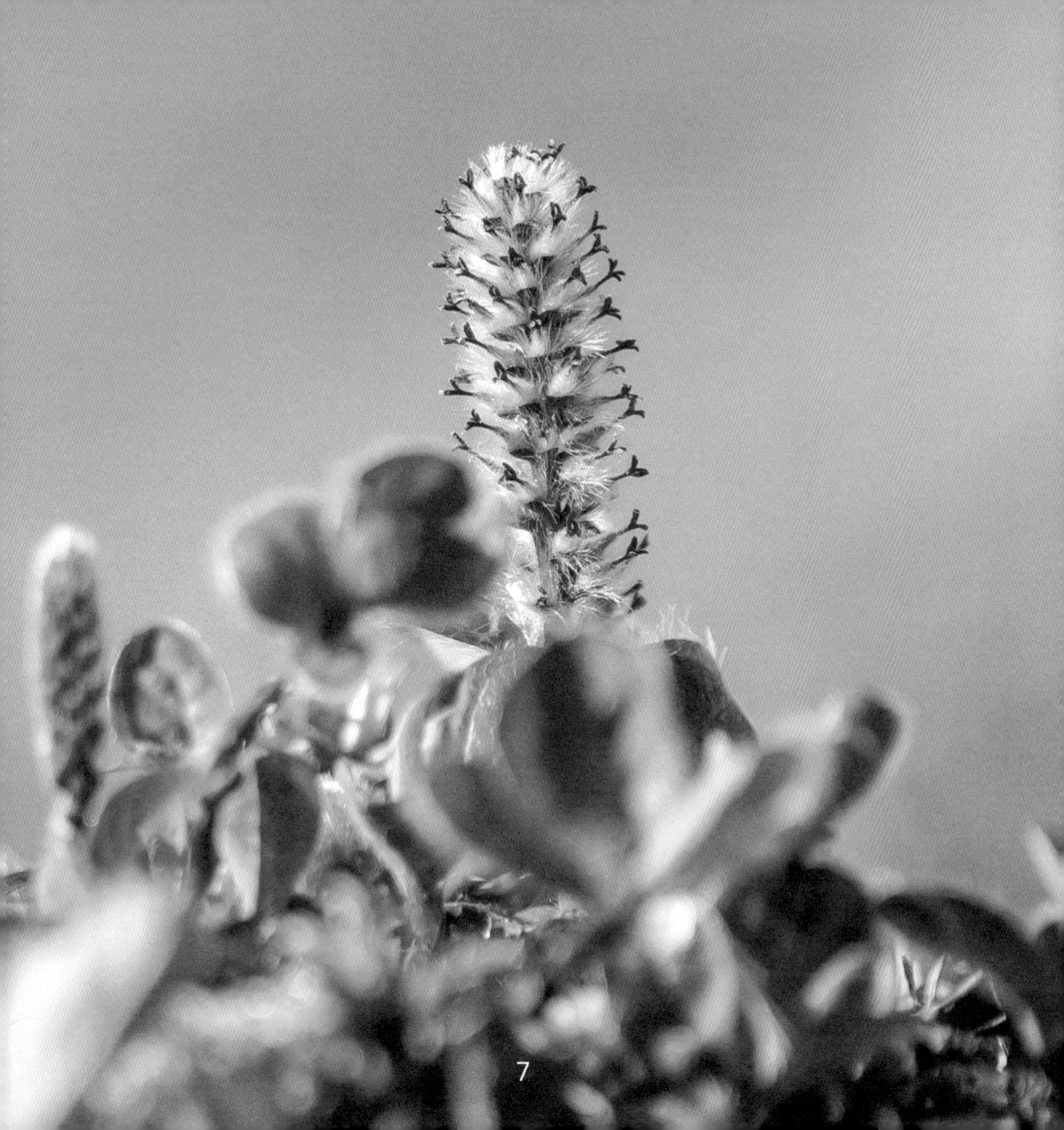

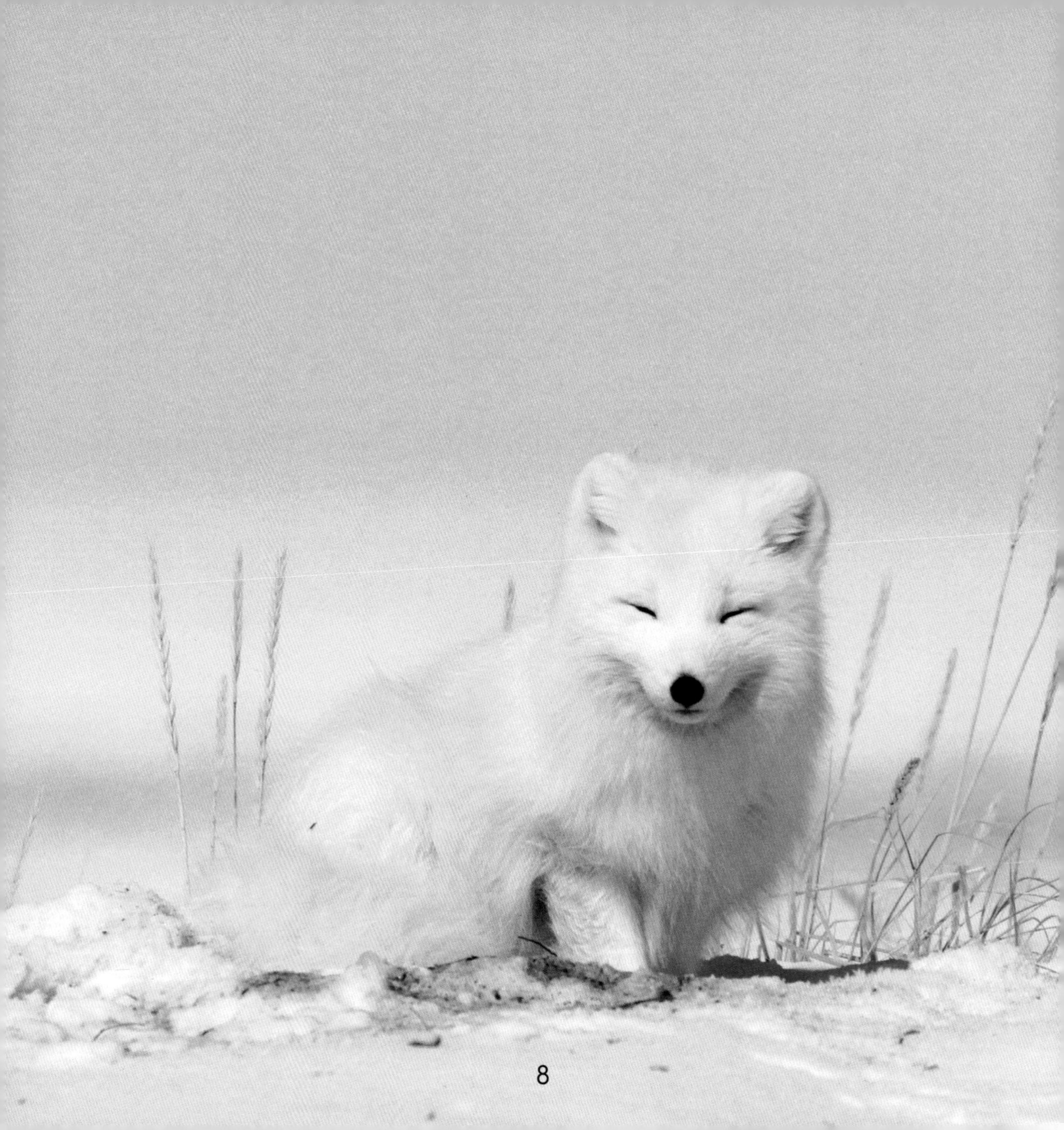

This is a fox.

This is a polar bear.

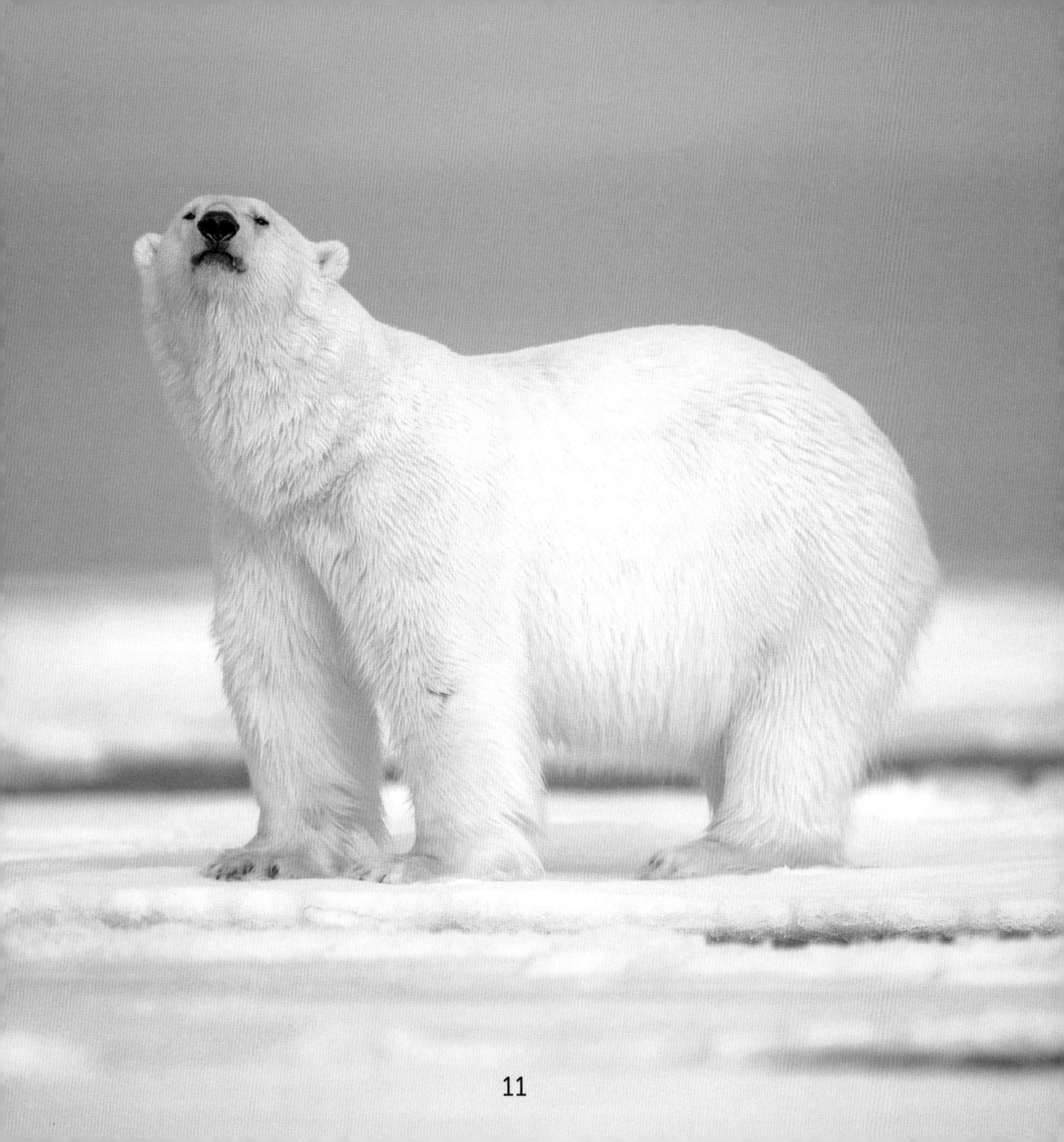

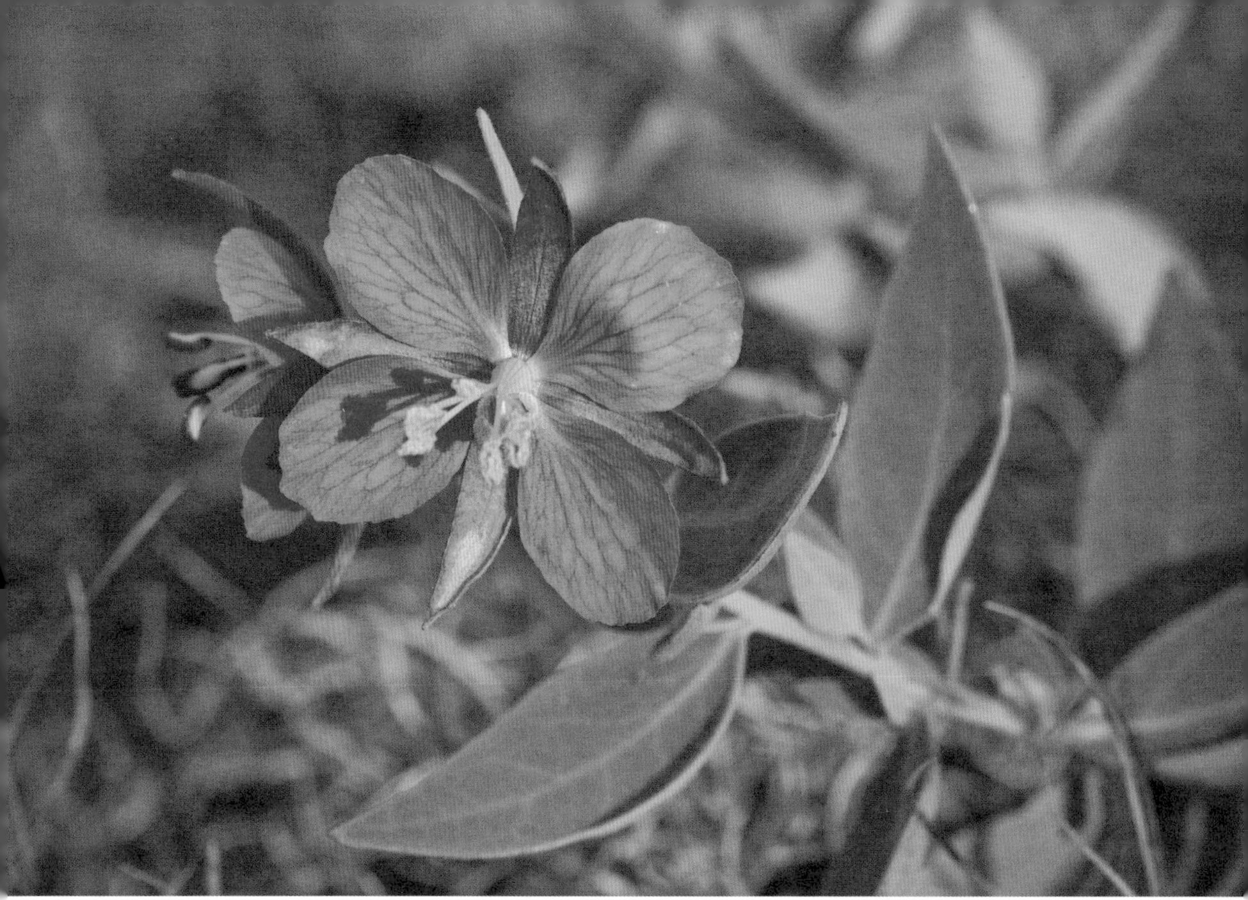

This is dwarf fireweed.